PACAL
A Maya King

Fiona MacDonald

PACIFIC
LEARNING

© 2004 **Pacific Learning**

© 2001 Written by **Fiona MacDonald**

Photography: The Art Archive: pp. 3, 4, 24; The Bridgeman Art Library/ British Museum: p. 17 (bottom); Corbis/Sergio Dorantes: p. 5 (right); Corbis/Macduff Everton: p. 19 (top); Corbis/Danny Lehrman: p. 20; Corbis/Charles & Josette Lenars: p. 6; Explorer/J. P. Courau: p. 11 (top left); Peabody Museum, Harvard University/Hillel Burger: p. 8; South American Pictures/Robert Francis: p. 19 (bottom); South American Pictures/Tony Morrison: pp. 7, 22, 23, 25, 27 (bottom right); South American Pictures/Chris Sharp: pp. 15 (top), 31 (lower left); Werner Forman Archive: pp. 9, 10, 17 (top), 27 (top right); Werner Forman Archive/British Museum: pp. 11 (middle right), 12, 13, 14 (bottom right), 15 (bottom left), 16; Werner Forman Archive/National Museum of Anthropology, Mexico City: • Title page, pp. 7, 14 (top left), 18, 20, 26. Front Cover: Werner Forman Archive/National Museum of Anthropology, Mexico City; Back Cover: Corbis/Sergio Dorantes

Illustrations are by Jeff Anderson, Stefan Chabluk, Antonia Enthoven, Celia Hart, and Tony Morris

U.S. edit by **Rebecca McEwen**

This Americanized Edition of *Pacal, a Maya King,* originally published in England in 2001, is published by arrangement with Oxford University Press.

13 12 11 10 09
10 9 8 7 6 5 4 3 2

Published by
Pacific Learning
P.O. Box 2723
Huntington Beach, CA 92647-0723
www.pacificlearning.com

ISBN: 978-1-59055-367-1
PL-7314

Printed in The United States.

Contents

Who Was Pacal?

Pacal was king of Palenque, a kingdom in Mexico. He belonged to the Maya, a Native American people who still live in the same region today. Pacal was born in AD 603 and died in AD 683, when he was eighty years old.

Pacal became king in AD 615. He ruled for sixty-eight years. While he was king, Palenque grew very rich and powerful.

The ruins of Palenque city

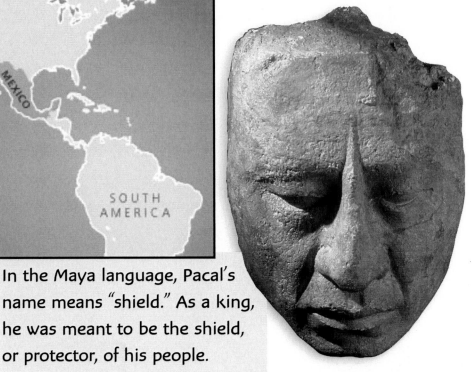

Pacal's death mask

In the Maya language, Pacal's name means "shield." As a king, he was meant to be the shield, or protector, of his people.

During his lifetime, Pacal was well-known as a strong ruler. Today, he is famous for his splendid **tomb** and the treasures buried there.

Pacal's body was placed into a **pyramid**-shaped **temple**, which became overgrown by trees after Palenque was abandoned around AD 900. Pacal's tomb lay forgotten until it was rediscovered in 1952.

Pacal's Family

Pacal's father was probably never the king of Palenque. Instead, he was a noble who belonged to the royal family. We know more about Pacal's mother. Her name was Zak Kul.

Pacal with his mother and grandmother

Maya mothers shaped their babies' heads by binding them gently between two wooden boards. This molded the soft bones of babies' skulls as they grew. To the Maya, a flattened forehead was a sign of beauty and also of very high **rank**.

Some historians think that this head is a portrait of Pacal. His forehead has been flattened and pushed back.

Some historians say that Zak Kul took control of the kingdom, and ruled it herself like a king. This was very unusual. Rulers had always been men. Maya people believed that kings had special powers, which were passed from father to son.

Pacal's grandmother was also strong and ambitious. Together, the two women plotted to make Pacal king.

Chosen to Be King

Most Maya kings had several wives and many sons. There were often quarrels among them over who should be the next king.

Before making a decision, kings probably looked for a boy who was strong, brave, and smart. They may have looked for signs among the stars and planets in the sky. They may also have asked advice from powerful people at the royal court.

This wall painting shows a boy being chosen to be the next king.

Maya kings held special ceremonies to announce which boy would rule after they died. They hoped this would prevent any quarrels. They also asked the gods to bless the boy chosen to be king.

At the ceremony, there was loud music and wild dancing. Enemy soldiers captured in battle were killed as a **sacrifice** to the gods. The Maya people believed that the gods needed regular gifts of blood, or else the world would come to an end.

We do not really know how Maya rulers chose boys to be future kings, but, somehow, Pacal was chosen. In AD 615, when Pacal was only twelve years old, the old king died. Pacal became king.

🁫 Ruler, Warrior, Priest

Like other Maya kings, Pacal was a ruler, a warrior, and a priest.

Ruler

As a ruler, Pacal passed new laws and made sure that royal officials did their jobs well.

Warrior

As a warrior, Pacal had to defend his city from attack. Sometimes he started new wars to capture enemy soldiers for sacrifices. A king who took many prisoners won great respect.

This **plaque** shows a king in royal robes.

A Maya king ready for war

A king with captives

Maya cities often fought one another. Warriors armed with spears and war clubs marched into battle. They shouted and made horrible faces while army musicians played loud war trumpets. Yet Maya soldiers did not kill their enemies immediately. Instead, they captured them to kill them as sacrifices to the gods.

Priest

As a priest, Pacal made sacrifices of humans and animals. These were offered to the gods. He was helped by other priests and **scribes**. Pacal also made offerings of some of his own blood to the gods. Maya people believed that the gods would help them in return for gifts of royal blood.

Blood sacrifices, like the one shown on page 13, were only made on important occasions, such as when a new king came to power.

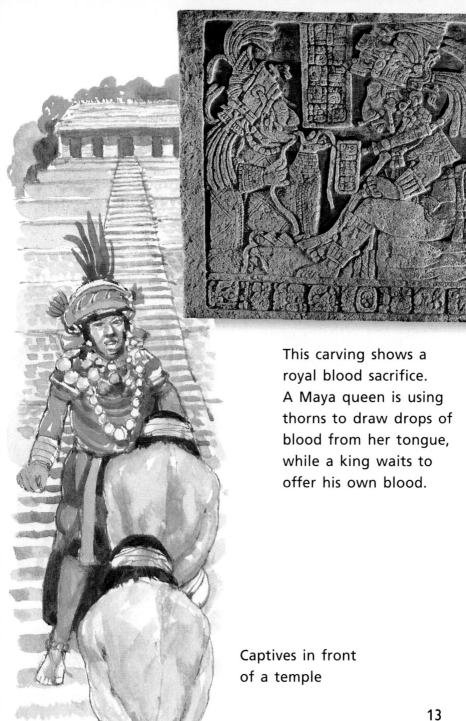

This carving shows a
royal blood sacrifice.
A Maya queen is using
thorns to draw drops of
blood from her tongue,
while a king waits to
offer his own blood.

Captives in front
of a temple

13

Rewriting History

Maya scribe

Pacal knew that he had become king in an unusual way. He wanted people to forget this, so he, or someone else, made up a myth. According to the myth, Pacal's mother, Zak Kul, was really the Moon Goddess in disguise.

The myth claimed that she had given birth to all the other gods, and to many kings. This meant that as her son, Pacal would be half-man, half-god, just like all the other Maya kings.

14

A Maya kneeling in front of an ancestor-spirit

Four kings carved on an altar

Ancestors are members of your family who lived long ago. Maya people believed that kings had the power to talk with their dead ancestors, either by offering blood or by chanting and dancing. They also believed that dead royal ancestors turned into gods.

The god of corn

As soon as Pacal took the throne, he began to do everything he could to make sure that the Maya people would let him keep the throne and pass it on to his sons.

Right away, he ordered artists to create stone carvings and paintings showing that his power really did come straight from the gods. In a way, for all sixty-seven years of his rule, the artists of Pacal's time rewrote history, and even changed Maya mythology.

Maybe this is why people today know so much about Pacal. Much of the remaining artwork in Palenque tells the story he wanted the world to believe.

There are many clues to help us learn about Maya times. Buildings, stone carvings, statues, wall paintings, and pottery have all survived.

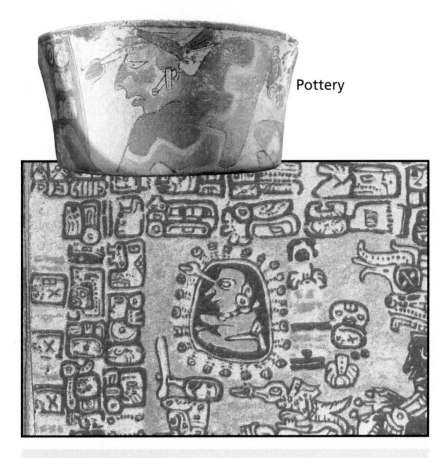

Pottery

Picture-writing

The Maya were the only Native Americans to invent a complete system of writing. Maya scribes wrote using glyphs (picture-symbols). They painted these in folding books, on pottery, and on walls. They also carved glyphs on buildings and statues. Many **monuments** in Palenque have the names of kings, and the dates they ruled, carved on them.

🔲 Pacal's Monuments

All Maya kings hoped to be remembered after they died. To help remind people about their lives, they used to pay for fine monuments, such as statues, palaces, or temples.

At Palenque, Pacal ordered the building of many monuments. One of the main buildings was a grand new palace in the city center. It was decorated with carvings of his ancestors and of men who had been captured and were waiting to be sacrificed. Pacal also ordered new stone temples, a massive tomb, and a new home for the royal family.

A Maya dancer

During Pacal's reign, Maya builders and engineers invented new ways of making buildings both stronger and lighter inside. They also designed a new canal to bring water to the city.

This palace, in the center of Palenque city, was built for the royal family.

Carvings of captive men at Palenque palace

 Pacal's Tomb

Of all the monuments that Pacal had built for himself, perhaps the finest was a huge mound, shaped like a pyramid, with a temple on top. Today, it is known as the "Temple of the **Inscriptions**" because it is decorated with carvings and glyphs. These show scenes from Pacal's life, and pictures of his eldest son.

Pacal's tomb

Pacal's jade
death mask

This temple was Pacal's tomb. The building
of this tomb began while Pacal was still alive.
His sons finished it after his death.

When Pacal died in AD 683, his body was
dressed in a necklace and earrings of jade (a
semiprecious green stone). Then it was
sprinkled with cinnabar (a bright red powder).
A beautiful jade mask covered Pacal's face.
Maya people believed all of these preparations
would **preserve** Pacal's body forever.

Pacal's body was placed inside a massive stone coffin, and lowered into a burial chamber deep inside the temple mound. The coffin was covered with a huge stone lid.

In fact, this lid is so large it weighs five tons, which isn't too surprising considering that the entire coffin weighs fifteen tons. The coffin was so heavy, it was set on its base before the temple was even built. Then the walls of the temple were built up around it.

On top of the lid is a carving of Pacal. He is falling down a large tree, which was a symbol for life, and then into the **underworld**.

Temple of the Inscriptions

Pacal's burial chamber and tomb.
You can see the carved stone coffin lid.

🏛 Pacal's Homeland

Most Maya people lived in rain forests. It was hot all year round, with heavy rainfall from May to October. In the south, there were mountains. To the north of the rain forests, there was a dry, dusty region near the coast.

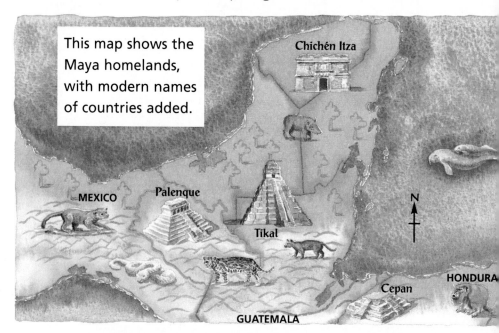

This map shows the Maya homelands, with modern names of countries added.

Chichén Itza

MEXICO

Palenque

Tikal

N

Cepan

HONDURA

GUATEMALA

Their rain-forest home was rich with wild fruits and nuts. The Maya people hunted deer, pigs, rabbits, snakes, and jaguars. They planted corn, beans, and pumpkins in clearings.

Maya families lived in small, single-story houses. The walls were made of wood or mud, and the roofs were thatched with dry grass.

Maya clothes were simple. A woman would wear a loose dress, and a man wore a strip of material wrapped around his hips. Men and women decorated their faces with tattoos, and arranged their hair in topknots.

A traditional Maya house

Maya Civilization

Pacal's city of Palenque was just one of many cities in the huge Maya lands. These lands were divided into many separate kingdoms. Each kingdom had its own big city.

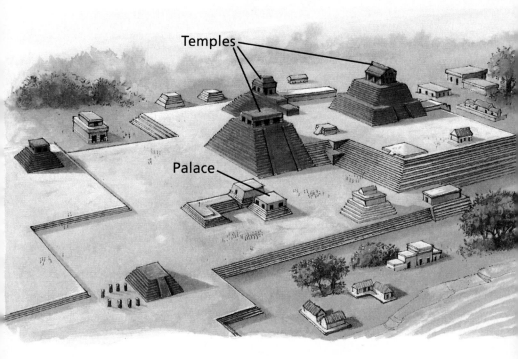

Temples

Palace

At the center of each city, there was a large open space. It was used for religious ceremonies, music, and dancing. Temples and royal palaces stood nearby.

Maya cities and villages were linked by roads and trails. These roads were used by traders and by armies marching off to war. Maya kingdoms often fought one another.

Each Maya kingdom was ruled by a king. Nobles, warriors, priests, scholars, and scribes were next in rank. Kings and nobles lived in the city centers. Ordinary people, such as farmers and craftspeople, were in the lowest rank, and lived outside the city.

A Maya girl weaving today

Craftspeople created buildings, fine stone carvings, brightly patterned cloth, and painted pottery. Scholars studied the stars and math. Scribes wrote books in picture-writing, composed songs and poems, and recorded exciting myths and legends.

Discovering the Maya

For centuries, the Maya **civilization** was a mystery to people living outside Maya lands. However, in the past 100 years, historians have studied the remains of Maya buildings, statues, carvings, and paintings. They have figured out how to read Maya glyphs. They have made many exciting discoveries, such as Pacal's hidden tomb. They have talked to Maya people living today.

Now we know much more about Maya people who lived long ago.

You can see some of the most important events in Maya history in the timeline on the following pages.

Timeline

2600 BC   First traces of Maya
civilization.

1500–100 BC   Maya are ruled by
Olmecs – people from
southern Mexico.

AD 250–850   Peak of Maya power.
Maya kings rule all Central
America and eastern Mexico.

AD 615–683   Reign of King Pacal over the city
of Palenque.

AD 850–900   Maya kings' power collapses,
although many ordinary Maya
people survive, as do their
language and lifestyle.

AD 900–1530   Maya ruled by Toltecs, who were
people from northern Mexico.

AD 1532   Soldiers from
          Spain start
          to conquer
          Maya lands.

AD 1697   Spanish soldiers
          conquer
          Tayasal, the
          final free Maya
          city.

AD 1952   Pacal's tomb
          discovered.

A modern photo of
a Maya boy

Glossary

civilization – a group of people who live together in an organized way

inscription – carved writing

monument – a statue or building built to remind people of something

plaque – a flat piece of metal or pottery hung either for decoration or as a memorial

preserve – to protect against decay, keep something from rotting

pyramid – huge tombs that are more narrow on top than at the base

rank – a title or job that shows how important someone is

sacrifice – a gift offered to a god

scribe – a person who made copies of pieces of writing before printing was invented

temple – a place where people worship

tomb – a place, sometimes a chamber, where a dead body is buried

underworld – a place for the spirits of the dead

Index